AND THE CHILDREN
OF MEDJUGORJE
AND YOU

by
Judith M. Albright

ILLUSTRATIONS AND COVER
by
Susan Shanahan

Published by
THE RIEHLE FOUNDATION
P.O. Box 7
Milford, Ohio 45150

The publisher recognizes and accepts that the final authority regarding the apparitions at Medjugorje rests with the Holy See of Rome, to whose judgment we willingly submit.

—The Publisher

Published by:
The Riehle Foundation
P.O. Box 7
Milford, Ohio 45150

Copyright © 1989 The Riehle Foundation.

Library of Congress Catalog Card No.: 89-62765

ISBN: 1-877678-05-8

MARY
AND THE CHILDREN
OF MEDJUGORJE
AND YOU

by
Judith M. Albright

DEDICATION

This book is dedicated to Sheila, Michael, Robby, Bridget, and Brian and to all the children of Mary.

THE LADY ON THE HILL

ONE day, in the little village of Medjugorje, Ivanka and Mirjana went for a walk. They were walking by a hill. Ivanka looked up and saw a shape of someone floating on a cloud.

"Look! It's the Virgin Mary!" she exclaimed!

"The Virgin Mary! It couldn't be! Do you think the Virgin Mary would appear to us?"

Mirjana shook her head and kept walking. "Come on, Ivanka."

Poor Ivanka didn't understand what was happening. She wanted to stay and look at the lady on the hill but her best friend, Mirjana, was walking away.

Finally she decided to follow her friend.

"I'm coming. Wait for me," she said sadly.

The girls were walking past Milka's house when Milka called to them.

"Ivanka! Mirjana! Will you help me get the sheep and bring them home?"

"Of course we will!" said Ivanka quickly. She new they would pass the hill where she had seen the lady. Maybe Milka would look and see her too!

The three girls hurried along. Ivanka was so happy and excited. All she could talk about was the lady on the hill.

"There she is!" cried Ivanka. "It's the Madonna holding Baby Jesus!"

All three girls saw her. They were so surprised. They felt happy, confused, and afraid, all at the same time. They also felt an inner peace which could not be explained.

The girls watched the lady. She was far up the hill but they could see that she was holding something in her arms. Ivanka was sure it was Our Lady with Baby Jesus.

The girls wanted to get closer but they were afraid. They could not believe their eyes. They didn't know what to do.

"Let's pray," said Mirjana. The girls knelt down on the dirt road and began to pray.

Just then Vicka came along and saw her friends kneeling in the road.

"What are you doing?" she called. She thought they were looking at a snake.

"The Madonna!" the girls shouted as they pointed toward the lady on the hill.

Vicka was afraid. She ran away. Her shoes fell off but she kept running.

Vicka met two boys, both named Ivan. They were carrying some apples they had picked. Vicka told them what had happened at the hill.

"Calm down!" they told her, "We'll go back with you and see what's going on."

Ivanka, Mirjana, and Milka were still praying in the middle of the road.

"Look up there!" Ivanka pointed.

Vicka and the boys looked up and saw a light. Gradually the light turned into the form of a lady. The younger boy became very frightened and ran away.

They were all confused. Then the lady motioned to them to come closer. But they didn't dare. Finally the lady disappeared.

The girls helped Milka get the sheep. Then they went home. They told their families and friends what they had seen but no one believed them. Some laughed and made fun of them.

Ivanka, Mirjana, and Vicka each had a grandmother who believed them. Their grandmothers told them to pray the Our Father, Hail Mary and Glory Be to the Father seven times.

When they went to bed that night, each child said a special prayer to Our Lady.

QUEEN OF PEACE

THE next day Vicka said, "Let's climb up the hill. Maybe the lady will come back."

"Oh! Yes!" said Ivanka.

"Maybe we can get closer to her this time," said Mirjana.

"I am not afraid anymore," said Ivan. "I will go with you. I won't run away this time."

"If you see anything, come and get me," said Maria. She was Milka's sister. "Milka wants to go but she has some chores to do."

"Okay," promised her friend Vicka.

Ivan, Vicka, Ivanka, and Mirjana started up the hill. They were nervous yet so excited. They could hardly wait to see what was going to happen.

A few of their friends went with them.

The hill is hard to climb. It is very steep and rocky. There are thorn bushes growing all around.

Suddenly, they saw a flash of light.

Vicka thought, "I must get Maria!" She ran back calling her friend.

Maria came quickly. Her little cousin, Jakov, ran after her.

The light flashed again! The six children, Ivan, Vicka, Ivanka, Mirjana, Maria, and Jakov, almost flew up the hill as if they had wings!

Vicka was barefooted but the sharp rocks did not hurt her feet. Somehow, she kept up with the others.

They all fell to their knees at the same time. Little Jakov landed in a thorn bush but was not even hurt.

All six children were kneeling and looking at Our Lady.

"Praise be to Jesus!" she greeted them.

She was the most beautiful person they had ever seen. They all loved her immediately. They had a great inner feeling of love and peace as they looked at Our Lady and listened to her voice.

Ivanka always believed that the Lady was the Virgin Mary. She never had any doubts. She was the first to see Our Lady. Now she was the first to speak with her.

"My mother died two months ago. Is she in Heaven?" she asked.

"Yes, your mother is in Heaven with me," said Our Lady. "She wants you to obey your grandmother and be good to her."

"Why did you come here?" asked Mirjana.

"I have found many believers here," replied Our Lady. "I want to ask for peace and love among all mankind."

The children said the Our Father, Hail Mary, and Glory Be seven times. Our Lady prayed with them, all except for the Hail Mary's. She smiled lovingly at the children as they prayed. She told them to also say the Apostles' Creed.

"Please, say these prayers every day," she said in her gentle manner.

Later she told them, "I am the Queen of Peace."

Her final words that day were, "Go in the peace of God."

The six children had talked with Our Lady! Then she disappeared. They knelt and prayed. The people who had followed them knelt and prayed too.

BLESSED ARE THEY WHO BELIEVE

T HE next day, three big flashes of light were seen on the hill of the apparition. People could see the flashes from miles away. It was as if Our Lady was calling everyone in the parish.

All of the people rushed to the hill with the children. Everyone knelt and prayed.

"Praise be to Jesus!" said Our Lady.

Jakov asked, "Who are you?"

"I am the Blessed Virgin Mary," she replied.

"Why did you come here?" asked Ivan. He could not believe someone so beautiful would come to their hill.

"There are many believers here," said Our Lady. "I want to be with you to call the world to peace with God and with each other."

From this answer the children knew that the Blessed Virgin Mary was not only talking to them, but to the whole world through them.

All of the people gathered there were very happy. Only the six children had seen Our Lady, but everyone knew in their hearts that she was there. They prayed and sang songs.

Finally, Our Lady said, "Go in the peace of God." Then she disappeared.

Each day the people would go to the hill of the apparitions to pray and to be with the six children when Our Lady appeared. Even though the people could not see the Blessed Virgin Mary, many believed that she was there.

Mirjana once asked Our Lady for a sign so that all the people would believe that she was appearing to them. Mary answered, "Blessed are they who believe but do not see."

GO OUT AND PROTECT THE CHILDREN!

THE six children would climb the hill of the apparitions every day. The crowds of people kept getting bigger and bigger. The police finally came and said, "You cannot meet on the hill to pray. All praying must be done in the church!" They stopped the people from going up the hill.

The Pastor of St. James Church was Father Jozo. He was worried about the children. He knelt in the Church and prayed to God for help. "What should I do?" he asked.

Suddenly he heard a loud voice say:

"GO OUT AND PROTECT THE CHILDREN!"

There was no one else in the Church! Father Jozo opened the door of the Church and looked out. He saw the children running toward him.

"Help! Father!" Ivanka cried out.

"The police are after us! Please hide us." begged Maria.

The children ran into the open arms of the priest. Father Jozo hid them in a room at his house. Then he went back outside by the church.

"Have you seen the children?" asked the police.

"Yes," answered the priest truthfully. He knew that he could not tell a lie. He was afraid of what would happen next.

To his surprise, the police turned and hurried away. They did not ask him any more questions.

TO JESUS THROUGH MARY

AFTER the police left the village, the people went to the church to look for the children.

When Father Jozo saw all the people looking for the children, he knew what to do. He invited them into the Church for Mass. Our Lady had led the people to her Holy Son, in the Holy Mass.

Father Jozo became a messenger for Our Lady. He helped the children spread her words to the rest of the world. Father Jozo preached about the love of Jesus and His loving Mother.

People came from all over to hear him speak about God and the messages from the Virgin Mary.

He said Jesus loves us so much that He sent His Mother to earth to help us. She wants to take care of us and love us. She wants us to live in peace and be happy with God. She is teaching us how to love by finding God's peace within ourselves and then seeing it in others.

Father Jozo said that Our Lady is very happy when we pray and she especially likes us to say the Rosary. She encourages us to forgive others and to offer up little sacrifices to God for the conversion of sinners, for non-believers, and for the souls in Purgatory.

It pleases her when we help others and do our work cheerfully. She asks us to read the Bible every day. Mary says that when we pray we become more beautiful, like flowers.

The people of Medjugorje liked the sermons Father Jozo gave. They began to go to Mass every day and to pray together as a family. The people have found peace and happiness in their hearts.

MIRACLES

MANY years ago, the villagers built a big concrete cross on top of the highest mountain near Medjugorje. One day the people could see the word "MIR," which means peace, written in the sky above Cross Mountain.

Some people have seen the cross light up at night. Other people have seen the cross disappear and a figure of Our Lady appear in its place. Mary told the children that she often goes to the cross to pray.

Many other miracles have happened in Medjugorje. People often see the sun dance and spin with beautiful colors in the sky.

Many people have been cured of physical illnesses while others have had spiritual conversions. People find peace in Medjugorje.

It is a place where many graces are given.

WHEN THE CHILDREN SEE MARY

PEOPLE from all over the world go to Medjugorje. They go to Mass, Communion, and Confession at St. James Church. They climb the hill of the apparitions and Cross Mountain. They walk around the villages of the parish. They visit the people and the children. They all pray together.

When it is time for Our Lady to appear to the children, everyone goes to the church. First they pray the rosary. When Mary appears, the children all fall to their knees at the same time and stare at the same place in front of them.

During this time, the children nod their heads and move their lips but no one can hear what they are saying. Their words are only for Mary. The children do not hear any sounds around them. They hear only Mary's voice, which they say is sweet and gentle. They do not see anything that is put in front of their eyes. They see only Mary, who they say is the most beautiful person they have ever seen.

When the apparition is over the priest says Mass. The church is full every evening for this Mass. Mary leads all of the people to her Son.

MESSAGES OF MARY

OUR Lady has been giving the children of Medjugorje messages for the whole world.

These are a few of the messages that are especially for children:

DEAR CHILDREN,
Today I am very happy because there are many who desire to devote themselves to me. I thank you. My Son, Jesus, wishes to give special graces to you through me. He is happy because of your dedication. Thank you for your response to my call. (5/17/84)

DEAR CHILDREN,
Your prayers have helped my plans to be fulfilled. Pray continually for their complete fulfillment. I beg the families to pray the family rosary. (9/27/84)

DEAR CHILDREN,
Today I invite you to renew prayer in your families. Encourage the very young to pray and go to Holy Mass. Jesus is giving you His graces in Mass. Let everyone who comes to Mass come with love and rejoice. (5/7/85)

DEAR CHILDREN,
I wish to call you to grow in love. A flower cannot grow without water. Neither can you grow without God's blessing. You should pray for His blessing every day so that you can grow normally and carry out your activities with God. (4/10/86)

DEAR CHILDREN,
I rejoice because of all of you who are on the way to holiness by your own testimony. Therefore, dear children, let your family be a place where holiness is born. Help everyone to live in holiness, especially your own family. (7/24/86)

DEAR CHILDREN,
Today I invite you to rejoice in the life which God gives you. Rejoice in God the Creator, because He has created you so wonderfully. Pray that your life may be a joyful thanksgiving, which flows out of your heart like a river of joy. Little children give thanks always for everything that you have, for each little gift which God has given you, so that joyful blessings always come down from God upon your life. (8/25/88)

MARY AND YOU

MARY comes each day as a loving Mother to guide all of her children. She says, "Pray, pray, pray, dear children. I am your Mother. I love you all. In prayer you will come to know my love and the love of God."

Mary's messages are very important for everybody. She tells us to be strong in our faith.

She tells us to pray, fast, do penance, forgive and love. If we do these things, we will find peace.

The messages are not just for the children of Medjugorje. They are for everyone. They are for you. They are your messages from the Queen of Peace.

Mary does all this because she loves you! It is so wonderful to have a loving Mother come to earth to gently guide us to holiness. She wants us to learn from her and to become a beautiful gift to God.

Our Lady is inviting us to listen to the words from Medjugorje and to follow them.

If we do what Mary asks, we will choose God. Then we too will "go in the peace of God." And one day Mary will say to us, "Thank you for your response to my call."

THE RIEHLE FOUNDATION

The Riehle Foundation is a tax-exempt non-profit foundation distributing Catholic literature around the world.

The foundation is deeply committed to making known Our Lord's message of love and peace. Today it seems that message is being delivered to the world through Our Mother, Mary, at Medjugorje; a continuation of the Fatima message delivered in 1917.

The Riehle Foundation publishes several books on Medjugorje.

Our Lady of Medjugorje
The story of the apparitions.
Color photos. 64 pages.
By Judith M. Albright ($3.50)

Our Lady Teaches About Prayer at Medjugorje
By Fr. Albert J. M. Shamon ($1)

Donations, though not required, are deeply appreciated. Suggested values for the above books are indicated.

To request copies of the above books or for additional copies of this book *Mary and the Children of Medjugorje and You,* please write to:

THE RIEHLE FOUNDATION
P.O. Box 7
Milford, Ohio 45150

All contributions are used for the publishing and/or distribution costs of providing spiritual material to a world desperately in need of learning more about and living in God's peace and love.